At the Counter

Soul Pause Journal

A Guided Companion for Reflection,
Prayer, and Everyday Faith

Laura Sharp-Waites

At the Counter Soul Pause Journal:
A Guided Companion for Reflection, Prayer, and Everyday Faith
© 2026 Laura Sharp-Waites
All rights reserved.

Published by Dare to Live Again Publishing
Newberry, South Carolina
www.DaretoLiveAgain.com

Dare to Live Again Publishing is an independent imprint devoted
to faith, soul care, and everyday spiritual formation.

First Edition

This book is offered for spiritual encouragement and refection. It is not intended as medical, psychological, or professional advice.

This book is offered for spiritual encouragement and refection. It is not intended as medical, psychological, or professional advice.

This is a work of nonfiction. This book contains personal reflections and stories. Names or identifying details may be changed to protect privacy.

ISBN: 979-8-9952325-2-0

Cover design by Laura Sharp-Waites
Interior design by Laura Sharp-Waites

Printed in the United States of America

This book was written at the counter, one ordinary day at a time.

A place for quiet reflection,
honest prayer, and the
ordinary moments of faith.

Dedication

This journal exists because readers asked for it.

Over time, many of you shared how the **Soul Pause reflections in *At the Counter*** became small moments of stillness in your day. Some of you began writing your thoughts in the margins, in notebooks, or on scraps of paper nearby.

You wondered what it might be like to have a space created just for that purpose.

This journal is for you.

Thank you for reading, reflecting, and gently encouraging this idea to grow into something more. May these pages offer you the same quiet invitation that inspired them in the first place.

Pull up a chair at the counter.

You belong here.

About This Journal

The ***At the Counter Soul Pause Journal*** was created as a guided companion to the devotional ***At the Counter: Spiritual Recipes for Faith in Everyday Life.***

Each chapter of the devotional includes a brief **Soul Pause**—a moment to reflect on where God may be meeting you in everyday life.

This journal gathers those moments into one place and provides space to write, pray, and explore your own reflections as you move through the devotional.

You may choose to write a little or a lot. Some days may fill a page. Other days may hold only a sentence or two.

Both are enough.

This journal is simply a place to notice what is already present—and to trust that God meets you there.

How to Use This Journal

This journal is an invitation to pause.

Each page begins with a **Soul Pause**, a simple question designed to help you notice what is already present in your life, your faith, and your ordinary days. There are no right answers here. The purpose is not to complete the pages perfectly, but to create space to reflect, pray, and listen.

You might choose to write a few sentences, fill the page, sketch a thought, or simply sit with the question for a moment. Some days you may feel drawn to write more. Other days, the quiet itself may be enough.

You can move through the journal however it serves you best. Some readers prefer to work through the **Soul Pauses** in order, while others open to a page that seems to meet them where they are. Either approach is welcome.

You may wish to begin your time with a short prayer or a deep breath. As you write, notice what rises to the surface: gratitude, questions, memories, hopes, or even places that still feel unfinished. All of it belongs here.

Return to the journal as often as you need. These pages are meant to hold your reflections over time, gently reminding you that God is present not only in the extraordinary moments of faith, but also in the quiet, ordinary rhythms of everyday life.

Some readers may also encounter these **Soul Pause** questions in study groups or book discussions connected with *At the Counter.* **Companion Leader Guides** are available for those who wish to explore the reflections in community. Whether you are journaling on your own or alongside others, these pages are simply a place to notice what is present and respond honestly. https://daretoliveagain.com/leader-guide/

You may also notice a section near the end of this journal called **Counter Companions**.

These pages are a collection of prayers for moments when reflection feels difficult, or when you don't quite have words of your own. You might find yourself turning to them on days that feel heavy, uncertain, or simply quiet.

If your time in these pages brings up deeper questions or emotions, you may find it helpful to listen, reflect, or simply sit with the companion podcast, **At the Counter with the Baking Pastor**, where these themes are explored in a conversational way

You can read them slowly, return to them often, or just let them hold the moment for you. Like the **Soul Pauses**, there is no right way to use these pages. They are simply here to sit with you.

Pull up a chair at the counter.

Take a breath.

Begin wherever you are.

At the Counter

Pull up a chair at the counter.

This is a place for ordinary moments, quiet questions, and the kind of reflection that often gets lost in the rush of daily life.

You do not need perfect words here.
You do not need to have everything figured out.
Just bring what is already present.

A thought.
A prayer.
A memory.
A question that hasn't found its answer yet.

God often meets us in the middle of the everyday—
in kitchens, conversations, pauses, and small acts of attention.

These pages simply give that moment a place to land.

So take a breath.
Pick up your pen.
And begin wherever you are.

Laura Sharp-Waites

Table of Contents

Opening Prayer

God of quiet moments,

As I open these pages, help me slow down enough to notice what is already here.

In the middle of ordinary days, unfinished thoughts, and questions I may not yet understand, remind me that your presence is never far away.

Give me honesty as I write, patience as I listen, and gentleness toward the places in my life that are still unfolding.

Let these pages become a small space of reflection, gratitude, and trust.

And in the simple act of pausing, help me remember that I am never alone.

Amen.

Soul Pause

What does your counter look like right now?

"Taste and see that the Lord is good;
blessed is the one who takes refuge in him." Psalm 34:8

Your Reflection

Soul Pause

What might it mean to invite God into
the ordinary moments of your day?

Your Reflection

Soul Pause

What makes up most of your ordinary days?

"And whatever you do, whether in word or deed, do it all in the name of the Lord Jesus..." Colossians 3:17

Your Reflection

Soul Pause

Where might holiness be quietly present,
even if you haven't noticed it yet?

Your Reflection

Soul Pause

When was the last time you noticed a deeper
kind of quiet?

"He says, 'Be still, and know that I am God.'"
Psalm 46:10

Your Reflection

Soul Pause

When was the last time you noticed a
deeper kind of quiet?

Your Reflection

Soul Pause

What might it be inviting you to hear or feel?

Your Reflection

Soul Pause

What simple tools or traditions carry meaning for you?

"Rejoice always, pray continually, give thanks in all circumstances…" 1 Thessalonians 5:16–18

Your Reflection

Soul Pause

*Where might God be present in the ordinary
things you reach for each day?*

Your Reflection

Soul Pause

Where are you being asked to hold space
than offer answers?

"Remain in me, as I also remain in you…"
John 15:4

20

Your Reflection

Soul Pause

What might it look like to stay present,
even when the outcome is unclear?

Your Reflection

Soul Pause

Where are you releasing the need to be perfect?

"My grace is sufficient for you, for my power is made perfect in weakness." 2 Corinthians 12:9

Your Reflection

Soul Pause

What broken or unfinished places in your life might be telling a deeper story of grace?

Your Reflection

Soul Pause

*What do you already have that you've
been overlooking?*

*"Moses stretched out his hand over the sea, and
all that night the Lord drove the sea back…"*
Exodus 14:21–22

Your Reflection

Soul Pause

Where might God be inviting you to take a first step, even if the way forward isn't clear yet?

Your Reflection

Soul Pause

Where in your life does it feel like nothing is happening right now?

"But those who hope in the Lord will renew their strength…" Isaiah 40:31

Your Reflection

Soul Pause

What might it mean to trust that growth is
still taking place beneath the surface?

Your Reflection

Soul Pause

*What does worship look like for you when
answers are delayed?*

*"Though it linger, wait for it; it will certainly
come and will not delay." Habakkuk 2:3*

Your Reflection

Soul Pause

How might you remain oriented toward
God, even while you wait?

Your Reflection

Soul Pause

Where do you feel tempted to rush right now?

"He who began a good work in you will carry it on to completion…" Philippians 1:6

Your Reflection

Soul Pause

*What might it look like to trust that God
is at work, even at a slower pace?*

Your Reflection

Soul Pause

What feels unfinished in your life right now?

"Because of the Lord's great love we are not consumed..." Lamentations 3:22

Your Reflection

Soul Pause

What might it look like to trust God with the process rather than demand completion?

Your Reflection

Soul Pause

What invitation keeps returning to you?

*"In their hearts humans plan their course, but
the Lord establishes their steps." Proverbs 16:9*

Your Reflection

Soul Pause

What trusted memories or tools might already
be supporting your next step?

Your Reflection

Soul Pause

Who might need quiet care right now?

*"For I was hungry and you gave me something
to eat…" Matthew 25:35*

Your Reflection

Soul Pause

What would it look like to offer nourishment
without needing the right words?

Your Reflection

Soul Pause

Where might a small kindness bring light
right now?

"Those who sow with tears will reap with songs
of joy." Psalm 126:5

Your Reflection

Soul Pause

What sweetness do you need permission
to receive?

Your Reflection

Soul Pause

*What might it look like to prepare kindness
ahead of time?*

*"The plans of the diligent lead to profit as surely
as haste leads to poverty." Proverbs 21:5*

Your Reflection

Soul Pause

*Where could freezer grace make showing
up a little easier?*

Your Reflection

Soul Pause

Where have you experienced quiet healing through shared presence?

"Share with the Lord's people who are in need. Practice hospitality." Romans 12:13

Your Reflection

Soul Pause

*Who might you invite, or accept an invitation
from, in this season?*

Your Reflection

Soul Pause

Where do you need softness right now?

"He tends his flock like a shepherd… he gently leads those that have young." Isaiah 40:11

Your Reflection

Soul Pause

What would it look like to let yourself
receive gentle care without apology?

Your Reflection

Soul Pause

*Where are you noticing small signs of
restoration in your life?*

*"Weeping may stay for the night, but rejoicing
comes in the morning." Psalm 30:5*

Your Reflection

Soul Pause

What would it look like to honor progress
without rushing what comes next?

Your Reflection

Soul Pause

*What small rhythm is returning to your
life right now?*

*"There is a time for everything, and a season for
every activity under the heavens." Ecclesiastes 3:1*

Your Reflection

Soul Pause

*How might you welcome it without pressure
or expectation?*

Your Reflection

Soul Pause

What is one small thing you can give thanks for today without needing to explain or expand it?

"Praise the Lord, my soul, and forget not all his benefits." Psalm 103:2

Your Reflection

Soul Pause

*Where might gratitude be inviting you to
slow down rather than speed up?*

Your Reflection

Soul Pause

*What joy did you inherit without
realizing it?*

*"Go, eat your food with gladness, and drink your wine
with a joyful heart, for God has already approved
what you do." Ecclesiastes 9:7*

Your Reflection

Soul Pause

*Where might celebration be inviting you to
show up fully again?*

Your Reflection

Soul Pause

Who has shared joy with you in a season
when it felt fragile?

"Rejoice with those who rejoice; mourn with those
who mourn." Romans 12:15

Your Reflection

Soul Pause

*Where might God be inviting you to let joy
be seen, even gently?*

Your Reflection

Soul Pause

*What blessing have you carried with you
through a hard season?*

*"The Lord bless you and keep you; the Lord make
his face shine on you and be gracious to you; the Lord
turn his face toward you and give you peace."*
Numbers 6:24–26

Your Reflection

Soul Pause

Who might need a quiet word of blessing
from you this week?

Your Reflection

Soul Pause

How do you usually feel about ordinary weeks?

"Who dares despise the day of small things"
Zechariah 4:10

Your Reflection

Soul Pause

*What might it look like to treat this one as
meaningful rather than something to get through?*

Your Reflection

Soul Pause

Where are you tempted to quit simply because something feels repetitive?

"Let us not become weary in doing good, for at the proper time we will reap a harvest if we do not give up." Galatians 6:9

Your Reflection

Soul Pause

What might it look like to trust that faith
is still forming you here?

Your Reflection

Soul Pause

What in your life are you tempted to dismiss
because it feels worn or ordinary?

"See, I am doing a new thing! Now it springs up;
do you not perceive it?" Isaiah 43:19

Your Reflection

Soul Pause

*How might God be inviting you to see
it differently?*

Your Reflection

Soul Pause

How have small acts of hospitality shaped your relationships or calling?

"Do not forget to show hospitality to strangers, for by so doing some people have shown hospitality to angels without knowing it." Hebrews 13:2

Your Reflection

Soul Pause

What do you already have that could be
shared in love?

Your Reflection

Soul Pause

Where do you resist being cared for, even when it's offered freely?

"Martha, Martha," the Lord answered, "you are worried and upset about many things, but few things are needed—or indeed only one." Luke 10:41–42

Your Reflection

Soul Pause

*What might change if you allowed yourself
to receive without explanation?*

Your Reflection

Soul Pause

*Where are you feeling asked to care for
more than feels manageable?*

*"How can I set this before a hundred men?" his servant
asked. But Elisha answered, "Give it to the people
to eat. For this is what the Lord says: 'They will
eat and have some left over.'" 2 Kings 4:43*

Your Reflection

Soul Pause

What simple offering might be enough
for this moment?

Your Reflection

Soul Pause

Where might flexibility serve love better than certainty right now?

"Invest in seven ventures, yes, in eight, for you do not know what disaster may come upon the land." Ecclesiastes 11:2

Your Reflection

Soul Pause

How can you offer nourishment without insisting
on one right way?

Your Reflection

Soul Pause

What helps you transition from giving to resting?

"Then, because so many people were coming and going that they did not even have a chance to eat, he said to them, 'Come with me by yourselves to a quiet place and get some rest.'" Mark 6:31

Your Reflection

Soul Pause

*Where might God be inviting you to pause
instead of pushing on?*

Your Reflection

Soul Pause

What helps you cool down after seasons of intensity?

"Like cold water to a weary soul is good news from a distant land." Proverbs 25:25

Your Reflection

Soul Pause

Where might God be offering relief rather than more responsibility?

Your Reflection

Soul Pause

Where are you tempted to rush what needs time?

"In vain you rise early and stay up late, toiling for food to eat— for he grants sleep to those he loves." Psalm 127:2

Your Reflection

Soul Pause

What might change if you allowed patience
to be part of your faith this week?

Your Reflection

Soul Pause

*What practices, people, or stories have kept
your faith alive over time?*

*"One generation commends your works to another;
they tell of your mighty acts." Psalm 145:4*

Your Reflection

Soul Pause

What might it look like to tend them again?

Your Reflection

Soul Pause

Take a slow breath. Unclench your jaw.
Let your shoulders drop. Imagine setting your
thoughts on the counter like a pile of ingredients.
You don't have to combine them.
You don't have to clean them up.
Just let them be seen and held.

"Do not be anxious about anything, but in every
situation, by prayer and petition, with thanksgiving,
present your requests to God." Philippians 4:6

Your Reflection

Soul Pause

*What future moment are you already
carrying today?*

*"Therefore do not worry about tomorrow, for
tomorrow will worry about itself. Each day has
enough trouble of its own." Matthew 6:34*

Your Reflection

Soul Pause

*What would it look like to set that
down, just for now?*

Your Reflection

Soul Pause

What is actually being asked of you in this moment, not the next one?

Your Reflection

Soul Pause

Where in your life are you being asked to
wait right now?

'Wait for the Lord; be strong and take heart
and wait for the Lord." Psalm 27:14

Your Reflection

Soul Pause

What would it look like to stay present
instead of forcing movement?

Your Reflection

Soul Pause

Can you trust that growth is happening
even if you can't see it yet?

Your Reflection

Soul Pause

*What would it look like to stop
explaining yourself today?*

*"In repentance and rest is your salvation, in quietness
and trust is your strength…" Isaiah 30:15*

Your Reflection

Soul Pause

*Where can you let your worth be
assumed instead of earned?*

Your Reflection

Soul Pause

*What happens if you allow this
moment to be enough?*

Your Reflection

Soul Pause

What small comfort do you keep within
reach for hard or heavy days?

"That each of them may eat and drink,
and find satisfaction in all their toil—
this is the gift of God." Ecclesiastes 3:13

Your Reflection

Soul Pause

Is there something simple you could prepare
now for a future moment of need?

Your Reflection

Soul Pause

Who taught you how to offer warmth, and how might you pass that on?

Your Reflection

Soul Pause

*Who comes to mind when you think
about sharing warmth?*

*"They broke bread in their homes and ate
together with glad and sincere hearts,
praising God." Acts 2:46*

166

Your Reflection

Soul Pause

What small gesture could feel natural,
not forced?

Your Reflection

Soul Pause

*Where might care already be moving
through you?*

Your Reflection

Soul Pause

What makes it hard for you to receive
help or kindness?

"Carry each other's burdens, and in this
way you will fulfill the law of Christ."
Galatians 6:2

Your Reflection

Soul Pause

*Who has offered care that you may have
quietly pushed away?*

Your Reflection

Soul Pause

What would it look like to say yes, even
when it feels inconvenient?

Your Reflection

Soul Pause

Where have you felt pressure to "make up for" care you received?

"For it is by grace you have been saved, through faith— and this is not from yourselves, it is the gift of God— not by works, so that no one can boast." Ephesians 2:8–9

Your Reflection

Soul Pause

*What would it look like to let gratitude
exist without obligation?*

Your Reflection

Soul Pause

Can you trust that love offered freely
is complete as it is?

Your Reflection

Soul Pause

*What ordinary practices help you
keep going?*

*"Whatever you do, work at it with all your
heart, as working for the Lord…"*
Colossians 3:23

Your Reflection

Soul Pause

*Where have you underestimated the strength
it takes to tend daily life?*

"Be still, and know that I am God."
— Psalm 46:10

Your Reflection

Soul Pause

*What would it look like to honor your
consistency instead of dismissing it?*

Your Reflection

Soul Pause

*Where are you being invited to begin
again, even quietly?*

*"Forget the former things; do not dwell on
the past. See, I am doing a new thing!"*
Isaiah 43:18–19

Your Reflection

Soul Pause

What small step could mark a fresh start today?

Your Reflection

Soul Pause

*What would it look like to release the
pressure to make it feel new?*

Your Reflection

Soul Pause

What small joy has found you recently?

*"Every good and perfect gift is from above,
coming down from the Father of the heavenly
lights, who does not change like shifting
shadows." James 1:17*

Your Reflection

Soul Pause

*Where have you felt a brief easing you
almost overlooked?*

Your Reflection

Soul Pause

How might you make room for these
moments without demanding more of them?

Your Reflection

Soul Pause

What memories return to you when
you're in the kitchen or at rest?

"I will remember the deeds of the Lord;
yes, I will remember your miracles of long ago.
I will consider all your works and meditate on
all your mighty deeds." Psalm 77:11–12

Your Reflection

Soul Pause

*Who taught you something that still
shapes you today?*

Your Reflection

Soul Pause

How might honoring those stories deepen your gratitude now?

Your Reflection

Soul Pause

*Where have you witnessed faith showing
up in unexpected places?*

*"Faith by itself, if it is not accompanied by
action, is dead." James 2:17*

Your Reflection

Soul Pause

*What moments in your life revealed care
you didn't know you needed?*

Your Reflection

Soul Pause

How might you honor those experiences
without needing to explain them away?

Your Reflection

Soul Pause

*Where have you noticed God's presence
in unexpected places?*

*"Where can I go from your Spirit? Where can
I flee from your presence?" Psalm 139:7*

Your Reflection

Soul Pause

How has your understanding of holiness
shifted over time?

Your Reflection

Soul Pause

What would it mean to trust that God
is already near, even now?

Your Reflection

Soul Pause

*How would your daily interactions change if
you trusted that God is already present?*

*"He has shown you, O mortal, what is good. And
what does the Lord require of you? To act justly
and to love mercy and to walk humbly with
your God." Micah 6:8*

Your Reflection

Soul Pause

Where might you slow down and simply stay?

Your Reflection

Soul Pause

What would it look like to release the
pressure to perform faith?

Your Reflection

Soul Pause

*Where might you take a small,
honest step today?*

"Keep your lives free from the love of money
and be content with what you have, because
God has said, 'Never will I leave you; never
will I forsake you.'" Hebrews 13:5

Your Reflection

Soul Pause

What fear feels lighter when you remember
you are not alone?

Your Reflection

Soul Pause

*How has trust already made you braver
than you realize?*

Your Reflection

Soul Pause

Where have you seen hope stay with you over time?

"May the God of hope fill you with all joy and peace as you trust in him, so that you may overflow with hope by the power of the Holy Spirit." Romans 15:13

Your Reflection

Soul Pause

What practices help you remain steady
when outcomes are uncertain?

Your Reflection

Soul Pause

How might you honor hope without
forcing it to be cheerful?

Your Reflection

Soul Pause

Where are you longing for certainty right now?

"Your word is a lamp for my feet, a light on my path." Psalm 119:105

Your Reflection

Soul Pause

*What might it look like to trust the next small
movement instead of the final outcome?*

Your Reflection

Soul Pause

*How has light already met you along
the way?*

Your Reflection

Soul Pause

Take one slow breath.
Imagine yourself seated at a table where nothing
must be earned and nothing must be proven.
What have you been holding too tightly?

"Come to me, all you who are weary
and burdened, and I will give
you rest." Matthew 11:28

Your Reflection

Soul Pause

*Where might release bring relief
instead of loss?*

Your Reflection

Counter Companions

Prayers for the Moments You're Living

There may be moments when you come to these pages without words.

Moments when reflection feels difficult, or when what you are carrying feels too heavy to sort through on your own.

These prayers are here for those times.

You can read them slowly, return to them often, or simply let them hold what you cannot yet say.

You do not have to find the right words.
You are already heard.

When You Feel Overwhelmed

Some moments feel heavier than you expected.

Prayer

God,
there is more here than I know how to carry.

Quiet what feels loud.
Steady what feels unsteady.
Help me release the need to hold everything at once.

Give me grace for this moment,
and trust for what I cannot yet see.

Amen.

When Nothing Feels Clear

Sometimes the next step feels hidden

Prayer

God,
when the path ahead feels uncertain,
remind me that I do not walk it alone.

Hold me steady in the not knowing.
Guide me in small ways I can follow.

Help me trust that clarity will come,
even if it arrives slowly.

Amen.

When You Are Waiting

Waiting can feel longer than expected.

Prayer

God,
in this season of waiting,
help me remain present instead of restless.

Strengthen my trust
when answers feel delayed.

Remind me that you are at work
even in what I cannot yet see.

Amen.

When You Feel Distant from God

Sometimes God feels far away.

Prayer

God,
even when I cannot feel your presence,
hold me close.

Meet me in the quiet places
where words do not come easily.

Remind me that distance does not mean absence.

You are still here.

Amen.

When You Are Beginning Again

Starting over takes courage.

Prayer

God,
as I begin again,
meet me without expectation.

Release me from the need to get it right.
Give me grace for small beginnings.

Remind me that new does not have to be perfect
to be meaningful.

Amen.

When You Need Rest

Rest can feel hard to receive.

Prayer

God,
teach me how to rest without guilt.

Quiet the voice that tells me I must keep going.
Help me trust that pausing is not failing.

Restore what has been worn down.
Renew what feels empty.

Amen.

When You Feel Stuck

Sometimes nothing seems to move.

Prayer

God,
when I feel stuck,
remind me that stillness is not the same as being lost.

Show me one small step.
Give me courage to take it.

Help me trust that movement can begin quietly.

Amen.

When Joy Feels Fragile

Joy can feel delicate in some seasons.

Prayer

God,
help me receive joy without fear of losing it.

Let me hold it gently,
without needing it to last forever.

Teach me to notice the small moments
where light still breaks through.

Amen.

When You Feel Pressured

Pressure can quietly build.

Prayer

God,
help me release what is not mine to prove.

Quiet the need to measure up.
Remind me that I am already held in your care.

Let me move through this day
with gentleness instead of pressure.

Amen.

When You Are Tired

Some weariness runs deep.

Prayer

God,
you see how tired I am.

Hold me in this moment.
Restore what has been drained.
Give me what I need for today, not everything at once.

Let your strength meet my weakness.

Amen.

When You Feel Alone

Loneliness can be quiet and heavy.

Prayer

God,
when I feel alone,
remind me that I am not unseen.

Draw near in ways I can recognize.
Surround me with your presence.

Help me trust that I am held, even here.

Amen.

When You Need

Courage

Some steps feel uncertain.

Prayer

God,
give me courage for what lies ahead.

Not all at once,
but enough for this next step.

Help me trust that you go before me
and remain with me.

Amen.

When You Need to Let Go

Letting go is rarely easy.

Prayer

God,
help me release what I am holding too tightly.

Give me peace in the letting go.
Replace fear with trust.

Hold what I release,
and hold me as I do.

Amen.

When You Need Hope

Hope can feel distant at times.

Prayer

God,
when hope feels far away,
help me notice even the smallest light.

Keep something steady within me
that does not depend on circumstances.

Remind me that hope can begin quietly.

Amen.

When You Feel Disappointed

Disappointment can linger quietly.

Prayer

God,
this is not what I hoped for.

Meet me in the space between expectation and reality.
Help me release what could have been
and receive what is, even if it feels unfinished.

Stay with me as I find my footing again.

Amen.

When You Don't Have Words to Pray

Sometimes words don't come.

Prayer

God,
you know what I cannot say.

Receive this quiet.
Receive this breath.
Receive what I am feeling, even without words.

Stay with me here.

Amen.

When You Are Carrying Too Much

Some days feel like too much to hold.

Prayer

God,
you see what I am carrying.

Help me lay down what is not mine to hold.
Give me wisdom to release what I can,
and strength for what remains.

Let me feel your care beneath it all.

Amen.

When You Feel Uncertain About the Future

The future can feel like too much to hold all at once.

Prayer

God,
I do not know what lies ahead.

Quiet my need to have it all figured out.
Help me trust the next step instead of the whole path.

Hold my future in your care,
and teach me to remain present in today.

Amen.

When You Are Carrying Quiet Grief

Some grief doesn't have words.

Prayer

God,
you see what I carry, even what I cannot explain.

Hold the places in me that still ache.
Be near to the memories, the loss, and the longing.

Let your comfort meet me gently,
without rushing what needs time.

Amen.

When You Need to Be Reminded You Are Held

Some days you just need to remember.

Prayer

God,
remind me that I am held.

Not because I have everything together,
but because your care does not depend on me.

Hold me in your presence.
Steady me in your love.

Let that be enough for today.

Amen.

Closing Prayer

Faithful God,

Thank you for the quiet moments held within these pages.

For the questions explored, the prayers whispered, the gratitude remembered, and even the places that remain unfinished.

Carry forward what has been noticed here.

Help the reflections written in these pages continue to shape how I move through ordinary days, trusting that your presence meets me there again and again.

Wherever I go from here, keep inviting me to pause, to listen, and to trust that you are already near.
Amen.

About the Author

Laura Sharp-Waites is a licensed minister, writer, and the voice behind The Baking Pastor. Her work weaves together storytelling, hospitality, and spiritual reflection, inviting others to encounter faith in the ordinary rhythms of everyday life.

Through her writing—and her podcast, **At the Counter with the Baking Pastor**—Laura creates space for gentle pauses, honest reflection, and conversations that meet people right where they are.

At the Counter: Soul Pause Journal grew out of the reflections found in her book ***At the Counter***, offering readers a place to slow down, write, and engage more deeply with their own stories of faith.

Whether through books, podcast conversations, speaking, or small group gathcrings, Laura's heart is to create spaces where people feel welcomed, seen, and invited to pull up a chair at the counter.

Companion Leader Guides and additional resources are available for those who wish to explore these reflections in community. https://daretoliveagain.com/leader-guide/

DARE TO LIVE AGAIN
FAITH · HOPE · RENEWAL
Newberry, South Carolina